KANSAS JOURNEYS

By Mil Penner & Carol Schmidt

Dedicated to V Lee, Gordon,
and Natasha

Design: Liz King
Editor: Mary Campbell Nielsen
Printer: Litho productions, inc.
Color Separations: Digital Color

ISBN 0-9615597-0-5

Printed in the United States of America

Introduction

Kansas Journeys is dedicated to the discovery of the subtle charm of Kansas found in the landscapes and the people of the state. The photographs and the authors' impressions seek to capture the unassuming beauty of the terrain and its inhabitants.

This is a personal study and a beginning exploration of the infinite variety within Kansas borders. Through 25,000 miles of travel, each physiographic area was explored, and each region evoked a different reaction. The journal material grew from traveling through the small towns and along the country roads as well as into the cities. Factual information was gathered from observation, from historic markers, from museums, and from books about Kansas. The homespun philosophies developed as each journey revealed links in the chain of being.

Kansas Journeys travels from the meditative atmosphere of the rounded Flint Hills to the productivity of the rich farmlands at the heart of the state; from solitude in the High Plains of western Kansas to the minute mysteries of nature in the woodland hills of eastern Kansas; from the once-brimming riverbeds to the sad disappearance of landmarks; from frivolous romance in the Red Hills to the ancient past of the Smoky Hills; from the nostalgia of old barns to the wild delicateness of the sand hills. Each place has its secrets, some uncovered by the camera lens, others seen in patient observation, still more revealed in quiet meditation. But even as the traveler watches, more secrets are being made; and no two Kansas journeys will ever be the same.

Kansas Geological Map

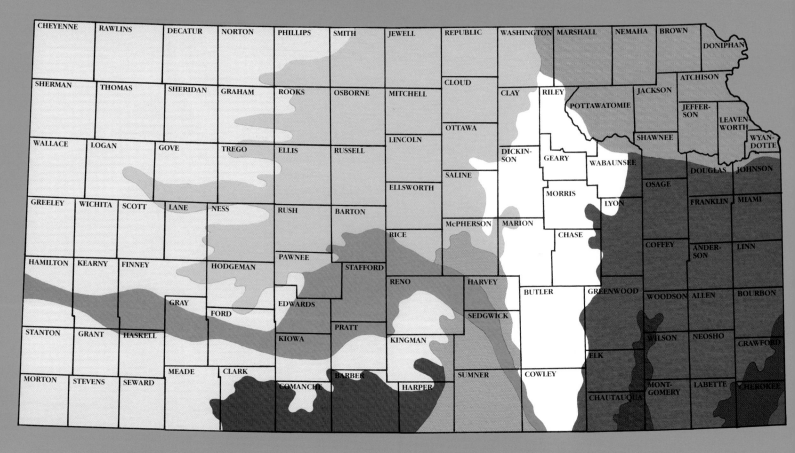

● High Plains
● Smoky Hills
● Arkansas River Lowlands
● Red Hills
● Glaciated Region

● Osage Cuestas
● Flint Hills Uplands
● Wellington-McPherson Lowlands
● Ozark Plateau
● Cherokee Lowlands
● Chautauqua Hills

Acknowledgment: Kansas GeoMaps,
Kansas Geological Survey,
Educational Series 4, 1983

Contents

The Flint Hills

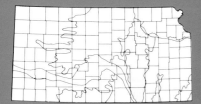

The opportunity to witness nature and its changes, however subtle or dramatic, is a gift to man.

When man produces his art, he imitates what he perceives in nature.

Both observing and imitating are essential to man's spiritual health.

The Flint Hills extend from near the northern border of Kansas to the southern border. At one time the Santa Fe Trail crossed them from Council Grove toward McPherson. Now Interstate 70 cuts through the hills from west of Topeka to Abilene, and the Kansas Turnpike follows them from near Wichita to Emporia.

The best way to see the hills, however, is to journey along the less-traveled routes, especially the gravel roads. From spring to fall cattle graze the bluestem and other native grasses. The gravelly soil layer over limestone is unsuitable for cultivation. Sometimes the grassland gives way to hidden streams or deep, fast-running rivers like the Cottonwood and the Walnut. Oak and cottonwood trees, sumac and wild plum bushes grow in the valleys. Prairie fires and a lack of rain in the hot summer months prevent tree growth, keeping the hills free to grow the tall prairie grasses as well as the abundant wildflowers from early spring to early winter.

Kansas State University is located in Manhattan, in the northern part of the Flint Hills. Just south and west of Manhattan, 8,616 acres have been set aside as a wildlife and tall grass preserve called the Konza Prairie. Maxwell Game Preserve is in eastern McPherson County. The rivers feed five man-made lakes or reservoirs: Council Grove, Tuttle Creek, Milford, Marion, and El Dorado.

Though it is difficult to imagine what the Santa Fe Trail must have been like when it crossed the Neosho River at Council Grove, the Flint Hills remain much the same as they were over one hundred fifty years ago. They constitute one of the largest areas of native grassland in the United States.

Opposite top: White evening-
primrose; early morning along
Cedar Creek. Below: Range land
near Highway 54 east of El Dorado.
Right: Reflections in the grass.

The predawn luminesence
played against the tall prairie
grass. The morning was reli-
giously serene. Then the glow
in the east brightened, and
a small, round sun appeared
through the freshness like a
pool of warmth on the horizon. It was a modest sunrise,
yet elegant, unassuming in
its simplicity like an ivory
rose carefully arranged in
a crystal vase.

The Flint Hills dawned around
us. Refractions in the dew
on the grass gleamed, splash-
ing a myriad of iridescent
colors on each blade. The
miniature world at our feet
glistened as if the fairies had
had a party the night before
and had neglected to extinguish their twinkling lights.

Journey of Discovery

Night hawks, first cousins to the whip-poor-will, performed their barnstorming courting rituals. High above us they voiced their nasal "peent, peent," then folded their wings and dropped to the earth like dive bombers, and with a sudden, deep whir at the end of their drops, spread their wings, to soar again and repeat, "peent, peent." Between their attacks and counterattacks of lovemaking, they rested sleepily on fence posts, only to fly again like Red Baron fighters.

An orchard oriole accompanied the rushing of Cedar Creek, with joyous outbursts and piping whistles. Like children, we dropped small pieces of flint rock into the clear water, leaving our grown-up concerns in the stream to be cleansed from our minds and becoming vulnerable to the world of beauty and adventure around us.

Magically, wild roses appeared along the roadsides. The reds and pinks cavorted in the wind, radiating their sweet perfume in every direction, leading us along the paths yet untraveled.

Journey of Discovery

Miles of barbed-wire fences stretched between posts of hedge or steel, creating abstract designs against the pastures, while clouds above formed their own creations—an infinite variety of common-place and fanciful images. Cattle grazed complacently or followed each other along cow paths that looked like roads on a map.

Amid sycamore and cotton-wood, their trunks concealed by wild plum bushes, a winding road met a wall of dense green and disappeared. As we rounded the curve, another secret rendezvous appeared, and then another. A stream across the road was to be forded with no bridge, only the rocky creek bed. All of this had been here for years, and yet suddenly I became aware of the incredible variety and magnitude of nature in a simple Kansas setting.

The road narrowed again, with grassy hills on both sides. An upland sandpiper whistled, flute-like, from a hedge post, its throat swelling to twice the size of its head. The bloom of a cactus caught my eye, its fluorescent petals appear-ing like velvet in a cushion of pins. A large trumpet bloom of yellow heralded the pres-ence of its fellow wildflowers, as if for that moment nature had called together a conclave of delicacies to treat anyone who would take the time to notice.

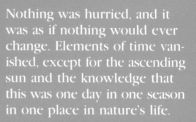

Opposite top: A large stone barn along Highway 50 between Florence and Peabody; a white evening-primrose closing for the warm part of the day; brown thrasher eggs. Opposite below: Sunset in summer near Newton. Left: The town of Clements: a mixture of spring wild flowers. Below: Two girls collecting earthworms near Matfield Green.

Nothing was hurried, and it was as if nothing would ever change. Elements of time vanished, except for the ascending sun and the knowledge that this was one day in one season in one place in nature's life.

Two little girls lazily collected earthworms in pop bottles, while their father mended a broken fence. "Going fishing in the pond," said the older of the two as she pointed eastward.

In a way, we went fishing too, though with no hook, no line, and no pole. Of course we didn't catch fish, we caught sights and sounds of the hills, soul food, to be stored in our memories and used at another time when our grown-up worlds again seemed to smother our senses.

Journey of Discovery

Below: Flint Hills in the spring; autumn along Cedar Creek; a frosting of ice and snow. Right: Cowbirds lay their eggs in other birds' nests. Right below: Flint Hills west of Junction City at dawn. Opposite top: Bridge over Cottonwood River near Clements; varieties of wildflowers bloom from early spring to late fall; large-flowered beardtongue.

We've been to the Flint Hills many times since our first trip, and whether the hills are covered with spring greens, summer whites and beiges, golden fall flowers, or a blanket of snow, they always reward us with their charm, quiet, and beauty.

There is a meditative quality, especially at sunrise or sunset. Perhaps it is because of the gentle slopes of the hills, which cast rounded shadows, or the rocky outcrops beneath the blue-and-white skies. Perhaps it is the variety of wildflowers that adorn the green pastures, or the abundance of birds: redwing blackbirds, meadowlarks, brown thrashers, cowbirds. . . . Perhaps it is the sight of many clear streams lined with trees or the less-traveled roads that wind over and around the rolling country. Whatever the reason, the hills are a place of comfort and strength.

In Search of the Buffalo

Fog hovered over the Flint Hills and softened the leaves and grass on an early morning in November. The air was crisp, damp. The low-lying clouds obscured the landscape and carried my thoughts to other places, other times. As Mil and I crossed the cattle guard on the west side of the animal preserve, four large buffalo moved across the road in front of us. Their heads were low and their breath rolled from their nostrils over their large, rounded backs. What we saw held us motionless.

Then, cautiously, we stepped out of the pickup to get a closer look. The animals were not interested in us. In fact, they didn't appear to notice us as they followed along the high fence that limited their territory. I wondered, were their spirits broken by captivity, or were they so sure of their power, their indestructibility that they cared little for the intruders, members of the species that had nearly brought their ancestors to extinction? Although they were moving slowly, they were soon swallowed by the fog, and my first close look at this powerful creature was gone.

We went quietly to the pick-up and drove to the preserve headquarters to meet Cliff Peterson, the manager. I eyed the Fish and Game emblem on Cliff's jacket. (I'd like to have one of those.)

Cliff let us ride with him while he was feeding range cubes to the herd from a small feed wagon pulled by his four-wheeler. We traveled across the pasture, sometimes on a road but more often through the amber, beige, and rust grass.

Opposite top: Cliff Peterson, the refuge caretaker; range cubes are fed daily in the winter. Opposite below: Buffalo number about 250 at Maxwell. Left: Annual auctions maintain proper herd numbers. Below: Bulls may weigh up to 1,900 pounds.

In Search of the Buffalo

Left: In the late 1800's the bison was almost extinct. Left below: Today the buffalo population is about 60,000. Below right: Maxwell also protects elk; sunrise at McPherson County Lake near Maxwell.

When we caught sight of a herd, some ten to twelve mothers and calves, I imagined another era when millions of these animals roamed the prairies—no fences, no white man.

The experience had the drama of a Wagnerian opera, only more basic, more earthy. Cliff honked the horn, and dark forms appeared on the horizon. "They have a pattern of grazing," he said, to explain how he knew where to find them. The buffalo moved closer and followed us. Cliff honked again as he pulled the rope to release the cubes, and more forms appeared.

Finally we stopped so that we could witness the full effect of the buffalo. Cliff warned us to be wary as these seemingly docile animals were not harmless. There was a smell of wet hair and a taste of dampness. As we stood among them, heavy, sharp hooves struck the soft earth and the buffalo made sounds that came from deep in their throats: primitive sounds both sensuous and mystical, adding to the feeling of Wagnerian romanticism.

To me, the grasslands were never so beautiful. The excitement and awe brought me as close as I would ever be to a time when the buffalo roamed unrestrained except by the elements and the American Indians, who believed the buffalo to be their brothers and took only what they needed. I shall not soon forget the voice of the buffalo.

Dawn at Cassoday

The dim first light of dawn outlined the hulking shapes of the "pots," the large cattle trailers whose parking lights looked like flying saucers in the heavy fog. The only other lights on the two-block main street came from the café windows, where the drivers waited for news that the cattle were ready for loading. The dense air muffled the drone of the idling diesel engines.

Cowboys out in the sprawling Flint Hills pastures would have to wait too until the heavy, gray shroud lifted, so that they could locate the cattle in the five-hundred-acre pasture.

Several hours were lost. The rancher was concerned, recalling the previous day, which had been full of delays and mishaps. He wanted this loading operation to go smoothly; he wanted to get the job done.

Finally word came: the cowboys had successfully rounded up the steers. Five trucks rolled out of town, in a caravan, to the holding pens several miles away. Without a hitch, the multi-decked pots were backed up to the chute one at a time, and the cowboys with their electric prods loaded forty-five head into each one.

By ten o'clock the trucks were ready for the two-hundred-mile trip to the feedyard. The rancher was pleased. The hills would be vacant until the early spring; they would be burned, and then a new growth of tall prairie grass would feed another crop of steers.

Opposite top: A cowboy's well-trained horse. Opposite below: Flint Hill cowboys; loading cattle with an electric prod. Left: Cattle corralled to load into pots. Below: Semi-trailer rig leaving for feed yard. Right: Cattle are herded six to eight at a time up the ramp; a loaded trailer ready to leave for western Kansas.

Chautauqua Hills

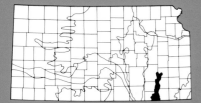

There is a natural balance in the wilderness, which, when appreciated, broadens man's understanding of freedom.

The Chautauqua Hills comprise a narrow band of hills and valleys, sixteen miles wide, extending sixty miles north from the Oklahoma border and including Toronto Reservoir in the extreme north. The hills were formed as deltas in an ancient sea about three hundred million years ago, when streams from higher elevations deposited eroded material. Four large rivers—the Verdigris, the Fall, the Elk, and the Caney—divide the region as they flow east.

Travel is limited; there are very few bridges, and most of the north-south roads are not surfaced. Six good highways cross east to west. Population is sparse, consisting of a half-dozen small towns and widely scattered ranches. As in other areas of Kansas, the small towns are disappearing. Country roads are unmarked and often impassable after rains.

Ranching, farming, and producing oil, as well as employment in nearby large cities, provide the economic basis for this region. As in other parts of southeast Kansas, the decline of industry due to depletion of natural resources has had an effect on employment opportunities. The Great Depression of the thirties and World War II marked the end of the industrial era.

Toronto Reservoir, with its wooded shorelines, provides facilities for picnicking, fishing, and boating. For the adventuresome who don't mind frequent dead ends, the rough country roads of the Chautauqua Hills offer intimate communion with nature.

Left: Wildflowers bloom among the oak trees and the bluestem grass; colorful new shingles on an old barn. Below: The early morning sunlight begins to burn off the fog. Right: Prairie groundsel blooms from May to June. Opposite top: Wood sorrel, used in soups and salads; a dry stream bed near Toronto Lake. Opposite below: A dandelion puff wet with dew.

The dense fog that hindered our travel to the Chautauqua Hills began to lift, creating shafts of light filtering through the branches of oak, pecan, and walnut trees to set in display the moisture-laden grass. Saturated dandelion puffs stood proudly on their stalks, barely strong enough to hold the added weight. Spider webs tightly secured to their moorings bobbed in the watery air. Nature's miniature world appeared magnified as if on a glass beneath a microscope.

As the sun's rays evaporated the low-lying clouds, vultures gathered, circling gracefully and evenly, their red heads and necks craning for the night's carrion.

Goldfinches darted to and fro, streaks of gold playing hide and seek, chattering as if they were planning a day filled with excitement, a journey no man would ever be able to imitate. Water ran beside the road and down the stair-step rocks amid a world full of variety in detail; it was breathtaking—a paradise—magically green, effervescent. Each dainty flower, each blade of grass encapsulated all of the beauty, the symmetry, the blemishes of nature.

In the Wilderness

Left: The mockingbird is an excellent mimic. Right: Roadside flowers near Coyville. Below: A lone American elm tree; a scissor-tailed flycatcher. Opposite top: A restored one-room schoolhouse; an old Standard station in Peru; an old log house along Highway 96. Opposite below: Yellow goatsbeard, also called western salsify.

A lone elm tree stood in a meadow full of wildflowers, and on its branches a mockingbird sang its repertoire, took its fanciful bow, and sang again. A rude audience of yellow-headed blackbirds busied themselves with their brown-bag lunches, more interested in food than in the concert. Two killdeer shrieked for attention, trying to lead predators away from their babies, camouflaged in the thick fenceline underbrush. A half-dozen scissor-tailed flycatchers replaced the mockingbird and flaunted their fashionable tails. Emily Dickinson would have loved this journey, had she not been so reclusive.

The woods were like seas of green voyaged by deer and other wild creatures. Tall, full-leafed oak clasped the ground, vulnerable to few forces except man's hand. Seasons of damp, dead leaves blanketed the rocky soil around their roots, saving the moisture for lacy wild roses and hundreds of clear springs.

The Chautauqua Hills are difficult to traverse, with rivers that have no bridges and roads that are subject to the whims of springs and temporary streams. It is wild country which defies taming—reason enough for its irresistible beauty. The natives say it is black-bear country, with bobcats and cougars as well; only the luxuriant hills, the stately oaks, and the deep rivers know for sure.

Ozark Plateau

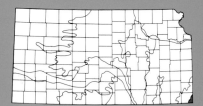

The mysteries and the beauty of nature are accessible to all who seek them.

Exploring the natural universe is a key to sustaining one's emotional, spiritual, and physical health.

A fifty-five-square-mile area in the southeastern corner of Kansas, the Ozark Plateau, with its steep, woodland hills, resembles the Ozark Mountains. It may look much the same now as it did 330 million years ago, but during the Pennsylvanian period it was covered by oceans and muddy sediments many times. Millions of years later, the earth's crust shifted, and mineralized water deposited zinc, lead, and other ores in openings in the limestone rock.

At the turn of the century, the economy of the area was based upon zinc and lead mining. Mining has since ended, but huge piles of chat can still be found around Galena and Baxter Springs. Twenty-two hundred acres of Cherokee County are undermined with shafts now filled with water, and the old mines are potentially dangerous, as they occasionally collapse. The abandoned mines may also be a cause of ground-water contamination.

Baxter Springs has a colorful past. It grew from a shack and a sawmill in 1850 to a cattle town in the 1860's. In 1870, with the arrival of the railroad, it became known as "the toughest town on earth." Today, near its historical museum, there is a wooden marker commemorating Chief Black Dog, an Osage Indian, who in 1805 established a trail from Oklahoma through Baxter Springs and across the Arkansas River at Oxford. Near the western edge of town, a monument has been erected as a memorial to the deaths of eighty-seven Union soldiers, massacred by Quantrill and his guerrillas.

Galena (named for the most common lead ore mineral) sprang up as a mining town in 1877, complete with Red Hot Street, lined with saloons and gambling houses. A railroad depot is now being converted into a museum to retain the flavor of Galena's earlier years.

Opposite top: The cattle egret inhabits meadows and marshes; Arkansas wild roses; the meadow-lark is the state bird of Kansas. Opposite below: The American elm is an excellent shade tree. Right: An Ozark deciduous forest; the pine tree's wooden flower. Below: A butterfly weed splashes color in a meadow; people once thought daisy fleabane kept fleas away.

Henry David Thoreau's New England cannot have been more beautiful than the lush green forests of oaks and the green meadows quilted with wildflowers in the Ozark Plateau. Farms merge into the steep hills, as if they grew there like the trees, and the cattle graze with snowy egrets guarding their backs. The woodlands flourish rough and rugged; streams descend from hidden sources; soft, green leaves shade nature's treasures.

Along the steep, curving roads, we frequently gave in to the temptation to stop, and we were rewarded each time. Across a placid meadow, two meadowlarks serenaded antiphonally. Butterflies trembled above the wild roses, and, hidden in the nearby trees, a bobwhite trilled.

In Schimmerhorn Park, we were greeted by a woman who had been hiking along the wooded trails. She directed us along a seldom-used path. "We are the forgotten part of Kansas," she said with a smile.

We walked slowly to explore the minute mysteries of nature: the veins on the elm leaf were like a map drawn on ancient parchment, a pine cone nestled like a wooden flower in the needles of its mother branch, and the patterns of light shone on the ground as if through a stained-glass window. Words of Thoreau came to mind: "Objects are concealed from our view, not so much because they are out of the course of visual ray as because we do not bring our minds and eyes to bear on them."

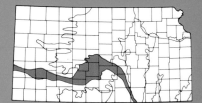

Although man can bend some of the forces of nature, destroy his own resources, and even extinguish whole species, he must consider the repercussions of what he does based upon what he observes. Man is a thinking animal. He must take care of the rivers, the wildlife, and the soil. He does not need to feel that such care is contrary to change or progress, as nature itself issues changes.

Man can guard against extinction by practicing appreciation and preservation.

The Arkansas River Lowlands extend from the Arkansas River to a width of up to fifty miles. The river, originating in the Rocky Mountains, has meandered across Kansas for 60 million years, leaving abandoned channels and areas of sand that are found in the lowlands along its present banks. Many of the sandy hills are much the same as they were two hundred years ago, although they are now peppered with oil wells and are used for cattle grazing. Irrigation and modern farming methods have turned some of the sand hills into productive farmland.

Coronado crossed the river east of Dodge City, and the Santa Fe Trail crossed it near Cimarron. Cattle were driven into Wichita along the Chisholm Trail, and later, as the railroad came west, Dodge City became the end of the trail for the cowboy. Now large cattle feed yards are found around both Dodge City and Garden City.

Today the Arkansas River flows through the cities of Garden City, Dodge City, Great Bend, Hutchinson, Wichita (the largest city in Kansas), and Arkansas City. A National Wildlife Refuge, Quivira is a part of the Arkansas River Lowlands. Quivira's salt water marshes are a refuge for thousands of migratory birds.

Wichita State University, Mid-America All-Indian Center, and many aircraft factories are located in Wichita. Hutchinson, known for salt mines and large grain elevators, hosts the Kansas State Fair and the National Junior College Basketball Tournaments and is home to the Kansas Cosmosphere and Discovery Center.

To the Sand Hills

Left: Watermelon is grown in small patches in the sand hills; sand hill plums picked for jelly or jam. Below: Chickasaw plums, commonly called sand hill plums; rosehips can be used to make tea. Opposite: Cottonwood trees in the Fall.

The sand hills are practically in my back yard, so I cannot claim one journey, one magnificent dawn or sunset, one morning or afternoon spent in discovery. I have been there many times, on picnics with the family and on camping trips with friends. The first journey Mil and I took together into the sand hills was in August. On the assumption that I must go "somewhere" to see "something," I wasn't sure I could feel an appreciation of sights so close to home.

We traveled straight west along the Valley Road south of Inman. Once in their midst, there is no mistaking the hills, though no signs designate them. We drove until the shrubs and vines along the sides of the road restricted our vehicle, and then we walked. We were surrounded by giant drifts of sand covered with flowers, yucca, and tall cottonwood trees. Juicy sand hill plums lined the path, and I picked some for jelly. I was careful to avoid the poison ivy that crept along the ground and climbed the cottonwoods. The bird calls produced a symphony of sorts: a pair of scolding blue jays, a bickering kingbird, a woodpecker hammering at a dead branch, a bobwhite calling softly in the distance. "Perhaps the birds are fond of sand hill plums, too, " I thought.

Opposite: Sand hill prairies are made of sand bluestem, sand love-grass, and little bluestem. Right: Monarch butterflies migrate over Kansas in September; domesticated geese on a morning jaunt. Below: A road becomes a trail.

To the Sand Hills

We went on. Fence posts lined the side of the road among the cottonwoods and brush. On the left was a pasture covered with white flowers. A windmill, signaling man's effort to utilize the coarse, dry sand, squeaked mockingly. Cattle crowded around it in the hot sun, swishing their tails at flies and silently waiting for the cool evening air to soften the grass. We walked west in silence until our trail became a road again, and then we turned back. I was glad to retrace our steps, to see again the delicate flowers that colored the hills, to hear again the symphony.

We have made other journeys along sandy roads which are little more than trails and often end abruptly in pastures or against rivers with no bridges to further our travel. One trip took us south of my home toward Burrton in the early fall, and we noticed the migrating Monarch butterflies on their way south. The sunflowers were covered with these beautiful insects as well as the Gray Haired Streaked butterflies and the bumblebees. Whole fields seemed to be in motion.

Right: A prairie rattlesnake; a snowy flower. Below: Quivira is a resting stop for migratory birds. Opposite top: Pelicans in flight over the Little Salt Marsh; Quivira National Wildlife refuge covers 21,820 acres. Opposite below: White pelicans are regular migrants to Quivira.

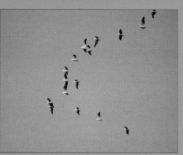

One of our favorite haunts in the sand hills is Quivira National Wildlife Refuge. Sunrise at Quivira is a magical time, the sky rich with golden light. In September, after witnessing a splendid dawn, Mil and I set off on foot to get a closer look at the pelicans camping on the Little Salt Water Marsh. It wasn't an easy walk. We skirted the mud flats and tried to avoid the tall grass, some of which was well over our heads. The blue water kept us from getting close to the birds. In the distance the water was white with pelicans, a sight I thought possible only in some exotic place along the coast of North America.

Later, as we trudged through some shorter grass, Mil and I talked about the waterfowl and questioned why we had never before taken time to explore this area. In places, the wild barrenness reminded me of the heath in Emily Bronte's *Wuthering Heights*.

"Stop!" Mil yelled, and something in his tone made me halt without question. In front of me, where my right foot would have landed, was a healthy, hungry-looking prairie rattlesnake. When we walked on, I realized what might have happened, and I thought, "So much for Gothic novels on the plains of Kansas."

Again in December, Mil and I visited Quivira. It had snowed, and a soft, wet, stilling blanket covered the trees and amber grass. A glistening white wind brushed my face as the geese sang their throaty chorus above me. The breeze would still and then rise a little as another flock of geese appeared. It was as if they were creating the wind with their beating wings. Deer jumped the fences and drifted through the plum thickets, their hooves padding against the damp, sandy earth as if they were wearing moccasins. At one point a pheasant scratched the white covering in front of me searching for food, his brilliant colors shocking against the white landscape, and then he vanished. Five bald eagles, perched in a cottonwood tree, kept watch.

Quivira is a delicate place. It is not, after all, the fabled Quivira, the richest city of the seven cities of Cibola, for which Coronado searched. It is instead a fragile treasure, a place for reflection, to be appreciated without compulsion.

Left: A white pricklypoppy. Below: The dried leaves of the pink mint-leaf beebalm can be used to freshen closets or drawers; sumac brightens the hills in October. Below right: A typical scene in the rolling sand hills. Opposite top: Harvesting milo near Nickerson; an Appaloosa; birds use berries for winter food.

Mil and I are often quiet on these journeys into the sand hills. There is peculiar mystery here, demanding silence and evoking a superstitious attitude in me. Sometimes I feel as if the mythical Greek gods, Zeus, Apollo, or Athena, may be just beyond the next hill. Leprechauns may be sitting in the cottonwood leaves, laughing at me. I make no claims to understand the mysteries of these hills. They are to me like a lady that looks into my heart, knows my secrets, and smiles.

When we travel the dirt roads and the "blue highways" of the Arkansas River Lowlands, we find many towns whose main streets are lined with hollow buildings. Here, as across Kansas, we have become accustomed to the sight of barns and houses with vacant faces. We have discovered historic landmarks that are being forgotten, and the Arkansas River itself may be in jeopardy.

When I walk a deserted street, I imagine the excitement when the towns were being platted and built. There must have been many Saturday nights when the town teemed with life: people busy talking, telling their stories, arguing, cussing, discussing politics and the world situation. . . .

What is true of the small towns is certainly true of the farmsteads. Many homes and barns have already disappeared. One can travel for miles now without seeing any homes where once there would have been several. The country is changing. The one-room school houses are extinct, and on modern farms steel buildings are replacing barns.

Opposite top: One of the many abandoned stores on Sylvia's main street; antique Avery tractor pulling a plow. Opposite below: In 1886, Sylvia had two elevators, three lumberyards, a bank, a brickyard, one newspaper, and eight other businesses; farmstead east of Dodge City. Left: Raymond post office. Right: An Amish girl. Below: Sunset near Fort Dodge.

Opposite: The old Oxford Mill. Left: Processing grain in the present Oxford Mill. Below: Tracks of the Santa Fe Trail east of Cimarron; cross commemorating Coronado's crossing of the Arkansas River.

Many landmarks are threatened. The Oxford Mill, in its small cove along the Arkansas River, is an example. Mil and I explored it on a bitterly cold January morning. One of the workers from the "new" mill, built in the thirties, graciously showed us the water-powered mill, erected in 1874. He took us through a maze of belts and pulleys, down some steps, and past a huge dynamo that was driven by the water turbine from 1934 to 1975. He then led us through a window and down the side of the building. "Too dangerous to go through the door," he explained. "The beams overhead are falling down." We circled some timbers and exited through another door. We were below the old mill-race, which stood some ten feet above our heads. I felt a mixture of admiration and regret as we walked out on the ice. I wondered what had happened to the families of the people who built the mill. What were their lives like when the wheel turned and powered the grinders? Does progress mean letting go of such accomplishments?

Along the Arkansas River

Left: Statue of a longhorn steer, El Capitan, in Dodge City. Below left: Arkansas River south of Great Bend. Below: Cheyenne Bottoms Wildlife Management Area is America's largest free shooting area. Opposite top: The Kansas State Fair is in Hutchinson; farm near Mulvane; grain elevator at Sylvia.

The river itself is disappearing. Two hundred and fifty miles upstream from Oxford, between Garden City and Dodge City, there is no water in the river bed. In fact, the river appears to be farmed west of Dodge City. At Great Bend the Cheyenne Bottoms are partially dry because the river has no water to feed them. There are places where the river is contaminated by effluent water and where acres of large cottonwood trees are dying. I wonder what the river was like near Cimarron in 1850 at the Santa Fe Trail crossing. Is the river, like the trail, to disappear, with a little marker saying, "This is where the Arkansas River was"?

We saw Canada geese wintering on the river in a residential area in Wichita! (I had to remind myself for a moment that this was not Quivira.) Hundreds of these large waterfowl are fed by the residents and are therefore not afraid of people. The geese walked on the melting ice, sometimes breaking through and creating a commotion until they situated themselves in the water. "Aren't geese related to swans?" I laughed as two geese landed near us. They skidded on their feet, their great clumsy wings flapping for balance, and then landed on their tails in a less-than-dignified positon.

Perhaps the geese set the tone of the afternoon for us as we went down the river to the junction of the Arkansas and Little Arkansas Rivers. The Keeper of the Plains, one of many statues in the city, was towering over us. The keeper was silhouetted against the setting sun, and to our east the sun lit the skyline, appearing like a stage setting freshly painted and ready for its first production.

"What's playing at Century II?" The twilight hour had arrived, and the city lights began to signal the beginning of night life: feasts at fine restaurants, movies and theatre, symphony, jazz, and ballet. It was time for play in the city.

Glaciated Area

The human record is brief compared to the history of the earth. The monuments man leaves behind are vulnerable to the forces which will complete the earth's story. It is both sobering and stimulating that man has yet to discover his role in this drama.

The red, brownish-red, or purple quartzite rock found in the Glaciated Area is evidence of the glaciers that covered the northeastern part of Kansas during the Pleistocene epoch. Glaciers carried this billion-year-old rock from South Dakota and Minnesota one million to two million years ago. As the glaciers melted they left a series of broad terraces along major stream valleys. Also left behind were vast areas of dry mud, which were subject to wind erosion and dust storms much worse than those of the 1930's.

Today, rolling hills, covered with pastures, farmland, woods, and cities, hide almost all traces of the chaotic glacial period. Atchison, Leavenworth, Kansas City, Lawrence, and Topeka lie along the Kansas and Missouri Rivers. Lake Perry sits seventeen miles northeast of Topeka.

The Glaciated Area contains the sites of the first white settlements and the first military outpost in the Kansas Territory. Both the Santa Fe and the Oregon Trails crossed the area. In the fight for statehood, from 1855 until 1861, four different constitutions were drafted—at Topeka, Lecompton, Leavenworth, and Wyandotte—before statehood was approved.

The largest and oldest state university in Kansas is the University of Kansas in Lawrence. Also in Lawrence is Haskell Indian Junior College.

Of the nineteen Indian reservations in Kansas during the 1840's only the Potawatomie, Kickapoo, Iowa, Sac, and Fox—all in the Glaciated Area—remain.

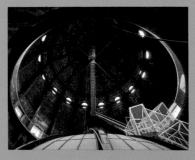

Left: Inside the dome of the state capitol above false dome; exterior of capitol dome. Below: Looking up from the bottom floor. Opposite top: One of the murals depicting Kansas. Opposite below: Brass and copper railings at the center of the capitol; the capitol in Topeka. Kansas became a state January 29, 1861.

Threads of the old and the new, the ancient and the contemporary, were woven through our journeys in the Glaciated Region. We followed a segment of Lewis and Clark's 1840 journey along the Missouri River. We touched the stones of the first territorial capitol at Lecompton and climbed the boulder-covered hills near Wamego. We saw the Indian reservations, a decaying railway depot in Leavenworth, and the thriving metropolitan areas in Wyandotte and Johnson Counties.

Our first stop was in Topeka, at the southern edge of the region. When I saw the dome of the capitol, I remembered my first trip to the top of the rotunda. It was on one of those grade-school outings when I was eight years old. I thought each step up was bigger then the previous one, and my feet had to reach a little higher each time.

Construction of the capitol out of Fort Riley limestone began in 1867, and today it is one of the most beautiful buildings in the country. To me it is as impressive as it was when I first saw it, but now I admire the stair and balcony railings of brass and copper, the murals depicting the history of the state, and the statues of heroes and heroines of the past: aviatrix Amelia Earhart, newspaper editor William Allen White, and President Dwight D. Eisenhower. I was not surprised to see the bulletin board next to the governor's office covered with birthday greetings sent by grade-school students. "Some things don't change much, do they?" I commented to Mil. "Do you suppose those children had to make copies of the state seal, with its *ad astra per aspera*, like I did?"

As we traveled on to Lawrence, I read a little history. The bitter proslavery-antislavery battle in territorial Kansas and the subsequent decision to be a free state anticipated the Civil War and freedom for the slaves. "Maybe from this, Kansans have concluded that as Kansans think, so does the nation," I observed.

When we arrived in Lawrence, the sounds of the campanile were reverberating on the campus of the University of Kansas. The university was established five years after statehood, and it is handsomely set among the Glaciated Hills.

In Johnson County, new high-rise office buildings, condominiums, and hotels stretch for five miles along Interstate 435. "Perhaps this is where all the people from the rural areas are going," I thought, "to a new age of high-tech commerce." The modern skyline of the College Boulevard area clashed with the older, weathered buildings of downtown Kansas City. Here as we walked the streets of old Kansas City, I tried to imagine the city as it once was, but I couldn't help noticing a policeman going by every three minutes or so.

From Kansas City we followed the route of Lewis and Clark up the Missouri River to Fort Leavenworth. The old fort, established in 1827 and situated on the top of a hill overlooking the river to the east, was built to protect the Santa Fe Trail against the Indians. The town of Leavenworth, platted in 1854 by proslavery forces, was founded illegally on Delaware Indian Trust land.

Mil and I talked about our sometime dubious history as a state and as a country, recalling that our early education neglected the "other side," the perspective of the Negro and the American Indian.

Before reaching Atchison, we stopped at a grain elevator on the edge of the Missouri River, where barges are loaded with grain for shipment to the gulf. Mr. Gearhart, the assistant manager, offered to take us up to the top of the elevator—to give us a bird's-eye view of the river and of Atchison two miles upstream. At the man lift, Mr. Gearhart asked, "Who's first?" There was neither room nor power for all three of us to go up at one time. I volunteered.

The view was spectacular. All fear I might have had of the height (some 200 feet) was subdued by what lay below. The river was still spotted with chunks of ice but was to be open for barge traffic in early March. I could see Atchison and the place where Lewis and Clark shared a glass of whiskey with their men at the first Independence Day celebration west of the Missouri River.

The horizon, the plains, and the blue sky dominated the scene. All else was small in comparison. The road that we had just traveled was a mere trail. The town of Atchison was just a splash on the horizon.

Opposite top: Original pony express station near Hanover. Opposite below: Looking up the Missouri River from the top of a grain elevator. Left: The original Kansas territorial capitol at Lecompton. Right: Snowdrifts south of Marysville. Below: The Missouri River view from Fort Leavenworth.

Opposite: Dutch mill in Wamego. Right: A glacial rock in Potta-watomie County; the Beecher Bible and Rifle Church was established in 1862 in the "Bleeding Kansas" period. Below: A 1944 Union Pacific steam locomotive traveling through Marysville returning from the New Orleans World's Fair to Omaha, Nebraska.

BEECHER BIBLE AND RIFLE
CHURCH
1862

Journey in Time

On the ground again, we drove through the countryside and finally stopped to see the Dutch mill in a charming little park in Wamego. I was sitting on one of the large, reddish rocks along the drive when an old man approached me. "Do you know how old that mill is?" he asked.

"Over a hundred years," I smiled.

Picking up a stick, he drew a line approximately two feet long in the dirt, with a mark at one end representing 1985. "It was built in 1879," he said, as he made another mark five inches from the first. "Columbus discovered America about here." He drew a mark fifteen inches farther on the line. Then he asked if I knew how old the rock was on which I was sitting. I couldn't answer him.

"Over two billion years old," he replied as he drew an arrow at the other end of his line. "When I was in my twenties, I thought I was the smartest man this side of the Mississippi River. I was prepared to tackle whatever wrong I saw and make it right—you know, kind of like a John Wayne of the plains. When I reached fifty, I realized that there is more than one side to every issue and it depends on what slice of the world a person sees as to what stand he takes. At eighty, I found that most of us don't know much. Knowledge of these old pink rocks puts me in my proper place.

"You know, I'd have to draw this line to San Francisco if I wanted to give you the right perspective of their age. In fact," he said, his eyes twin-kling, "man has been on this earth for a time equal to about a mile and a half from here."

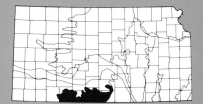

Man has been able to make his environment comfortable. He has the ability to protect himself from the elements and from changes in the weather. He need seldom feel the cold of winter, the heat of summer. Yet the coming of spring, to those who choose to experience it, is a blessing.

The Red Hills, or Gyp Hills as they are commonly known, are made up of deposits of brick-red shale, siltstone, and sandstone. The Plains Indians called them the Medicine Hills. Some of them, capped with gypsum and dolomite, are quite rugged, and roads through the mesas and around the buttes are sparse. Highway 160 from near Harper to fifteen miles past Ashland is a safe way to travel. For more adventure, take a side road like the one from Medicine Lodge to Sun City and Belvidere.

Medicine Lodge is the largest town in the area. Its one industry other than agriculture is the gypsum mill. It was once an active frontier town and has a colorful past. Carry Nation, the prohibitionist who often expressed her views in violent raids on open saloons, lived there. Hendry Brown, marshal of nearby Caldwell, led a bank robbery in 1884. Brown was shot and his three accomplices were hanged by a mob of angry townspeople.

Other towns in the Red Hills are Harper, Ashland, and Anthony. Runnymede was an English settlement near Harper; it has disappeared except for the remains of its tree nursery. The Medicine River, the Chikaskia River, and the Cimarron River all flow through the region. Many of the smaller towns are nearly deserted, and the people who remain seem to enjoy the solitude.

Ranching, wheat farming, and gyp mining make up much of the industry in the area. Signs along the highway point to the larger ranches. Hell's Half Acre (actually several acres of rough terrain) is on one of these ranches, and permission must be obtained to see it.

The Plains Indians, the Kiowas and the Comanches, believed the red hills and streams had spirits that helped cure illnesses and heal wounds. The Kiowas built a lodge at the fork of the Medicine River and Elm Creek. In 1867, near the Kiowas' medicine lodge, a commission from the U.S. government met with groups of Cheyennes, Arapahoes, Plains Apaches, Comanches, and Kiowas to sign a peace treaty. The treaty soon disintegrated when promised annuities failed to arrive and greater numbers of white settlers invaded the buffalo hunting grounds.

Opposite top: Magnolia blossoms in Medicine Lodge; red tulip in Harper city park; catkins from a cottonwood tree. Opposite below: Buttes west of Medicine Lodge. Right: These trees are the only evidence of Runnymede, the original church having been moved to Harper; painting by Agnes Nye of Runnymede as it was in the 1890's. Below: Hell's Half Acre.

The Arrival of Spring

In memory, the Red Hills dissolve into shadows and contours, like the view from a plane ten thousand feet in the air. The red earth is like blood in the green patches below. White and gold rock are like veins through the pastures, and everything seems to be softened by the strokes of an impressionist's brush.

Spring is the subject on this journey; spring and what it represents to anyone who feels the coldness of winter, who sees the naked outlines of trees against deep blue skies or who hears the crunch of footsteps in the snow. In spring, romance seems to emerge no matter how protected one is, no matter how busy one is with the complexities of living. Daily we have been concerned with, as Exupery's Little Prince says, "matters of consequence," when suddenly a simple bud or a crocus in bloom undermines our self-importance. Then, something snaps inside and we are "in love" with no reason, with no purpose, with no rightness.

The journey in the Red Hills began in Runnymede, a town built by an Irish flimflam man and a practical Englishman. I dare you to find Runnymede. Its life was short, some five years, and what remains is a grove of trees. Here was my first experience with spring this year. Beneath the budding branches, I could hear a ruddy, sandy-haired Irishman laughing, and I could see the Englishman's furrowed face as he made arrangements to buy, sell, or build.

Runnymede's green grass, suggesting frivolity, gave way to red-soil cliffs in Clark and Barber Counties. There I could smell the smoke from the Indian peace pipe and hear the war chants, see the red earth on the warriors' faces, and feel the drums beating messages of blood. The Medicine Lodge Peace Treaty is broken. No one admits to knowing exactly why. The wind sighs, oblivious, as the battle begins and the confrontation between two cultures is settled with weapons.

The Medicine River flows clear over the crimson soil. The rancher and the cowboy play the cattle game. The high bluffs, the buttes and mesas, the gyp hills belong to the rugged individual. Hell's Half Acre, with it's steep cliffs and sand sculptures carved by years of wind, rain, and turbulent water, feeds the bovine spirit. At one point I stood in "divide pasture" and could see some fifteen miles to the north. Someone's grandfather once owned this land, as far as the eye could see, part of the seventy-thousand-acre Robbins Ranch.

Frank Rockefeller (John D. Rockefeller's maverick brother) owned a three-thousand-acre ranch near the Robbins Ranch. I could hear the chatter of Eastern gentlemen and ladies beneath the Kissing Rock. I saw them pose astride their horses for their pictures on the back of Camel Rock. I imagined the personal railway cars, the ride to and from the station in the chauffeured limousines, the dances in the ballroom on the third floor of the Rockefeller mansion.

Spring issued a warning. Thunderclouds rolled from the southwest, threatening to drop torrents of rain that would flood our retreat from Hell's Half Acre.

We outran the storm and took shelter in a drugstore in Medicine Lodge. Here, the righteousness of Carry Nation boomed around us. She is locked in the cellar beneath us where she rumbles helplessly like the thunder. We laughed a little nervously, knowing that storms inside and out can be dangerous.

The storm in me was one of acknowledging the arrival of spring. My rational mind said that I was the same as I was yesterday. Nothing had changed. But there was an ache in my breast that I could not subdue, a moistening of the eyes that my intellect tried to interpret as hay fever, and a smile on my lips I could not erase. The sunset added its blessing to the Red Hills, and an elusive rainbow rimmed the sky overhead.

Opposite top: Longhorns on one of the many ranches in the Gyp Hills; Camel Rock south of Belvidere; thunderclouds over butte west of Medicine Lodge. Opposite below: Kissing Rock south of Belvidere. Right: Forsythia blossoms. Below: Brick street in Medicine Lodge after thunderstorm.

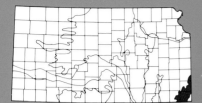

One man may be seen by his peers and by history as famous, another as eccentric. One man may be a success and his neighbor, a failure. Regardless of the label attached to an individual, each is more like the other than he is different.

The coal fields in the Cherokee Lowlands are called the Little Balkans, named after the Balkans in Europe because of the area's embattled political past and the fifty-two nationalities represented. The Little Balkans' inhabitants are descended from Italians, Germans, French, Belgians, and a variety of ethnic groups from the British Isles and the Austro-Hungarian Empire.

Here the history is different from that of any other part of Kansas. When railroads were built into the area, coal mining became an important industry in southeastern Kansas. Eastern industrialists and entrepreneurs established zinc, lead, and silver smelting, adding to the need for manpower. Southeastern Kansas became one of the leading industrial areas of the country at the turn of the century.

Coal was discovered at the surface of the ground by settlers, and the relatively flat terrain changed as the first strip mines opened during the early 1870's. Shaft mining was introduced in 1874 by the Scammon brothers, but underground mining again gave way to strip mining in 1950. Today there is little mining activity, and now strict laws require turning strip-mined land back to its natural state. Some of the older mined areas have been reclaimed for farmland, while the Kansas Fish and Game Commission oversees six thousand acres of the now rough and rolling terrain as a Mined Land Wildlife Area. Pits up to forty-five feet in depth are populated with fish and surrounded with dense undergrowth and vegetation.

Pittsburg, named after Pittsburgh, Pennsylvania, is the largest city in the area and is the home of Pittsburg State University, known for its unique School of Technology and Applied Science and its work toward improvement of various industries in Kansas. Columbus, the county seat of Cherokee, is the second largest city. The towns of today still bear the colorful names of the early mining camps: Arma, Franklin, Scammon, Roseland, Mineral, Cherokee, Frontenac, Weir, and Treece.

The Cherokee Lowlands puzzle me. They suggest absurdity, like clashing colors splashed on a canvas with no immediately apparent design. The landscape has an unnatural appearance, and yet trees, underbrush, and wildlife seem to be abundant.

When Mil and I turned off Highway 96 to the strip-mined land, I was surprised by the lush vegetation that surrounded the deep pools. I expected desolation, because I had seen a black-and-white winter photo in a geology book. Nature is reclaiming the land. Turtles were sunning themselves on old logs, and a cardinal scolded us.

Yet the remains of man's intrusion show through nature's veneer. The once-flat lowlands have been ravaged almost geometrically, as if a giant plow had turned the soil. There are hills of black discarded overburden showing signs of rapid erosion along their steep slopes. I was torn between a sense of relief that nature was at work and a gnawing apprehension that something was not right and may never be right.

When we saw Brutus, the giant power shovel, on the horizon, I admired its extraordinary size. I wanted to see it bite off a chunk of earth. I wanted to see the huge wheels turn, the tracks move, and the cables strain to pull. Now devoid of its engines and generators, it was like a skeleton.

Then I stood in front of the bucket that used to dig one-and-one-half train carloads of soil in a single healthy bite. In front of me was a trench as wide as a football field. I thought, "Et tu, Brute!" I was pleased that Brutus had joined the ranks of discarded machinery and would no longer abuse the earth.

Mil and I went in search of abandoned underground mines. We were curious and wanted the excitement of being in a mine shaft. What we found, instead, was an eighty-five-year-old man who had worked in one. He seemed happy to be alive, and, as he talked, I understood why. Life in the mine was not filled with excitement but with hard work and danger. He described picking at the coal vein under a three-foot-high ceiling and then shoving the coal out with his feet. I looked into the old gentleman's eyes, and I thought of a line from the country music song *Sixteen Tons:* "St. Peter, don't you call me 'cause I can't go; I owe my soul to the company store."

Opposite top: Green Elm school, at the Pittsburg Museum. Opposite below: A sunset near West Mineral; one of the 26 lakes of the Mined Land Wildlife Area; Brutus, the huge power shovel used to strip over-burden from the coal veins. Left: Black overburden stripped from a coal layer; a tufted titmouse. Right: Catalpa leaves. Below: Brutus over-shadows a pickup.

Left: Fishing for largemouth bass and channel catfish. Below: An abandoned strip-mining operation south of Pittsburg. Right: Folk art by Hance White. Opposite top: Canada geese grazing wheat; full moon over old coal mines.

There are no shaft mines left in Southeast Kansas, but, through the man we met, I felt as if I had experienced what life must have been like for him and his fellow workers and their families. I understood the strikes for more pay and better working conditions and the march of the Amazon Army (a miners' wives' protest); I wondered why I had never recognized this version of "Bleeding Kansas." People here did not bleed only over the issue of slavery, they bled in the mine fields and in the zinc and lead smelting plants. The very soil of Kansas bled with the extraction of coal in the early twentieth century.

Later, as I sat by a brook that bubbled over rocks, I reflected on the former mining towns we had seen in the area, skeletons like Brutus. Where are the grandsons and granddaughters of the miners now? Have we learned and progressed because of the miners' experience in the coal fields?

In Pittsburg, I watched the faces of the people along the streets. They were not so different from the faces in other towns. They didn't suggest more pain or more joy. In the downtown park, a family of three was having a picnic dinner. I thought of my own family. During lunch in an Italian restaurant, the television was turned to a popular soap opera, and I thought of some of my friends. Outside, the sun was shining, and everyone was going about his business. I was a little embarrassed by my earlier dramatic interpretation of the past.

Pittsburg was not much different from Hutchinson or Newton.

Symbols of the past are scattered throughout Pittsburg. The ornate entry of the Stillwell Hotel once welcomed industrialists and entrepreneurs, who arrived in their black hats and with their Eastern money to build an industrial state. It now stands empty and in need of repair. Harold Bell Wright's voice once boomed sermons in Pittsburg; his former home, now in a quiet residential area, is unnoticed. Hance White adorned his place of business, the Pittsburg Marble Works, with his heroes and heroines. Today the venerated faces, examples of folk art, are for sale. An empty bottle of Corona's Best, a southeastern Kansas bootlegger's product, stands in the window of an antique store.

Sitting on the edge of one of the strip-mined pools, I watched a canoe drift lazily along the bank. Two men alternated throwing their fishing lines into the still water. One of the men pulled in a large bass. I learned that, even if fish cannot survive below ten feet here, the fishing is good. Sometimes I see the pools as beautifully blue and clear, sometimes they appear to be brown. I have yet to discover which they are, and perhaps they are both.

Osage Cuestas

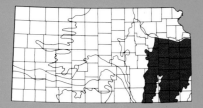

Man can use his experience to understand the present, but there is danger in remaining in the past.

The Osage Cuestas are named in part for the Osage Indians from Missouri, who used eastern Kansas as their seasonal hunting ground. As the white man settled in Missouri, the Osages were given southeastern Kansas in exchange for their homeland; but again, as the value of Kansas lands became apparent to white promoters, the Osages were removed to Oklahoma.

Cuestas are hills with a steep face on one side and a gentle slope on the other. They are made up of layers of shale, limestone, and sandstone that were deposited in shallow seas. Generally the steep slopes face east in the Osage Cuestas.

At the turn of the century, the abundance of shallow natural-gas wells in the region fostered the establishment of zinc smelters, cement plants, and glass factories. As the gas supply dwindled, these operations were abandoned. Today only a few cement plants remain.

Agriculture is more varied here than in other parts of the state. Wheat fields, dairies, irrigation, and grazing land on farms of all sizes can be found. Although woodlands, creeks, and hills divide the land into small fields, many of the smaller tracts have now been consolidated into large farms of a thousand acres or more. Many abandoned barns testify to changes in farming methods.

Old Fort Scott, a National Historic Site, is a reminder of Indian warfare, of "Bleeding Kansas," and of the Civil War. The fort is well restored and is maintained by the National Park Service. Emporia, home of William Allen White, is the location of Emporia State University.

Rivers in the Osage Cuestas are deep and swift. They were subject to frequent and severe flooding before dams and reservoirs were constructed. Many wooded areas, meadows, and wildlife refuges, such as the Marais des Cygnes and the Neosho Waterfowl Refuges, provide a haven for birds, animals, and wildflowers.

Left: In the spring, barn swallows build nests in dark barns. Below: Hay was stored in barns, cane and corn silage in silos. Opposite top: Amish children near Mont Ida; sheep are sheared in early spring. Opposite below: A barn built with cottonwood lumber.

Like bits of memorabilia, old barns are scattered across the countryside and hidden in the valleys of the Osage Cuestas. I wanted to savor each one. What is it about such buildings that causes outbreaks of nostalgia in rational people?

For some of us, who were fortunate to grow up with barns nearby, there are childhood memories of climbing high in the beams and rafters to raid pigeon nests for squab; of finding day-old baby kittens nestled in a dark corner; of smelling the soft hay in the winter; of swinging on the suspended ropes and then dropping into the mounds of dried prairie grass; of witnessing the birth of a calf or colt; of hearing banjo and fiddle music at a barn dance.

I remember discovering my brother asleep with his head resting on the belly of a half-grown, bottle-fed lamb. I recall the long afternoons we played cowboy and Indian (the hunter and the hunted), and the times I hid in the barn when I felt shy or lonely.

Old Barns

For those who know barns less intimately, perhaps sentiment is kindled by the warm, rich colors of wood smoothed by an animal's rubbing or a man's frequent touch.

Of course, barns were not built for children, and perhaps the nostalgia we feel as adults has to do with a departed era. The obsolescence of the barn symbolizes a way of life that once seemed permanent but has gradually disappeared.

Beloved by the painter, the barn is fast becoming anachronistic. There are no new barns in Kansas to my knowledge. Barns are seen in various states of health, from the decayed to the newly painted. Sadly, many are not used at all except for storing pieces of machinery and various antiquated items. Many others are being burned or razed.

There are barns with faces and barns with no faces. I wish they could tell me what they knew and what they had seen. There is a barn whose loft gave refuge to a family when the nearby creek overran its banks and threatened the house. I am sure there are not just a few haymows that lent themselves to adolescent love-making. The earthiness of the barn created an atmosphere for the farmer to share jokes and tall tales with friends.

As I entered one precarious old barn, a temperamental pregnant nanny goat eyed me suspiciously, and I hastily climbed into the haymow. I stood in the loft looking out over the countryside, and I was for a moment the little girl who sought refuge in the loft of her parents' barn.

Great barns, I have heard it said, have a heart and soul. Is it possible that the soul of a barn is a reflection of the owner's or the observer's soul? I stepped gingerly down the ladder and tested the wooden floor carefully as I walked quickly to the door. The wind was blowing through the cracks, raising dust, and I felt for a moment as if I were trapped. My memories at first had been comfortable, and then, as if lost in time, I had had enough of my own history, enough of nostalgia, enough of the protective haymow.

Opposite top: Nanny goat guards her territory; barns used to be the center of a farm's activity. Opposite below: A barn designed for a dairy herd. Below: One of the few remaining round barns in Kansas, northeast of Fort Scott. Right: The intricate interior dome of the round barn.

*Right: Prairie groundsel wild-
flowers; sunset near Howard. Below:
Phlox, one of the first to bloom in
the spring. Opposite top: A peach
blossom; a stream near Fort Scott.
Opposite below: Tiny white flowers
dot the deep grass; many geese
migrate over the area in the spring
and fall.*

A stone fence led me from the barn to the woods beyond. In the cool shade of the hackberry, black walnut, and sycamore trees, a stream polished the glistening rock in its bed. The wind gentled in the branches above. The wildflowers bowed politely, and I acknowledged them with a nod, as if I were in a Japanese tea garden and the purple and yellow flowers, Downy Phlox and Prairie Groundsel, were my host and hostess.

I nearly invaded a group of miniature white flowers, then stepped politely through lush green ferns and paused before a field of rippling pink. I sat beside my friend, the brook, and threw the last bits of nostalgia into its clear water and greeted the world around me.

The stream that flows to the river that flows to the sea invited me to follow. The stream becomes the Marais des Cygnes, marsh of swans, where a beautiful Indian mãiden and her betrothed warrior emerged from the river's mist as two beautiful swans, so the Osage legend tells.

High Plains

Man is closest to his God when he is alone in the great circle of life.

The High Plains area is a land of extremes. It is the hottest, the coldest, the windiest, the youngest, and the highest region of the state.

This large section of western Kansas and eastern Colorado was formed in the last sixty million years by the eastward flow of eroded rock debris from the newly uplifted Rocky Mountains. Water, in an underground layer of sand and gravel called the Ogallala Formation, is of great economic significance to the region.

Some early explorers referred to the High Plains as the Great American Desert, while others surmised its potential richness. The landscape is dominated by vast, open space, much of it intensely farmed and the rest rangeland. The flat appearance is often interrupted by abrupt valleys and basins such as the Big Basin, Lake Scott, and Clark County Lake.

Population is sparse in the region, often with only two or three small towns per county. People in rural areas are isolated from cities by long distances traversed by gravel roads. Severe winters and hot, dry summers combine with this isolation to make self-reliance a daily necessity in the lives of the farmers and ranchers here.

Economically, agriculture and the petroleum industry predominate. Cattle are grazed, fed in large feedyards, and slaughtered here, vertically integrating the production of beef. Grain to feed the livestock is produced on large, irrigated farms drawing water from the Ogallala Formation. In the south, the large Hugoton gas field, along with oil resources scattered over the whole region, is important economically to the area.

Major rivers are the Cimarron in the south, the Smoky Hill in the middle, and the headwaters of the Solomon and Saline in the north. The Republican flows across the extreme northwest corner from Colorado into Nebraska, reentering Kansas in Republic County. Besides the rivers, Norton and Webster Reservoirs and a dozen state and county lakes provide the limited surface-water resources.

Opposite: The word Kansas means "keepers of the rites pertaining to the wind." Right: A hill crest in the Big Basin in Clark County; near St. Jacob's Well along Highway 160. Below: An abandoned farmstead near Hugoton; St. Jacob's Well, a small pool that has never been dry.

Finding Mt. Sunflower

On the High Plains, sunrises and sunsets are like splashes of color dividing the earth and sky. Otherwise, the two meet to form a great circle around the place where one stands. The spacious, open terrain and the isolation it suggests are intimidating. At times a single tree, a lone house, or a prairie grain castle may be seen on the horizon, but the road ahead appears changeless, like a straight line leading to unblemished infinity.

Without warning, the road that was as straight and level as the path of an arrow dropped between white cliffs to a valley filled with teal-blue water. The horizon which formed the giant circle at our feet was much smaller and high above. The wind rolled over the slopes, rippled the lake, and gently rocked the boats of fishermen. Below the dam, cottonwoods and elms mocked the yucca on the ridge one hundred feet above.

A winding road led us up through the cliffs to the edge of the circle, to the endless prairie. A strong south wind greeted us, blowing dust devils across the fields. On the other side of the county, another valley enveloped us, and limestone fence posts led the way to St. Jacob's Well. Cumulous clouds raced above the natural rock wall, entertaining us with different poses like mime artists presenting their imaginary props. One particularly playful vapor directed us onto a steep incline where the road ended; the sky and a fifty-foot drop greeted us.

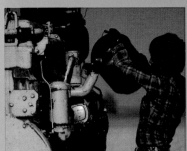

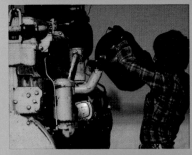

Finding another road, we returned to the land above and to hills dotted with yucca and scented with sagebrush. The wind blew furiously and incessantly. It divides the strong from the weak, sometimes draining strength and sometimes molding a brave spirit.

The earth flattened again, and I was startled and then delighted to see lush, green wheat. The wind whisked the air from the irrigated field and brushed its refreshing coolness across my face. For the most part, farming survives here because of the water which lies under the ground, but it is a resource that is being depleted. I struggled to balance an appreciation for progress and a love of nature. Even though I was distressed by the dryness of the Cimarron River bed, as I saw the rows of thirsty green plants I could not condemn the men and women who pump the water from the earth with their giant Caterpillar engines. Am I so different from them when I water my garden or my lawn?

Finding Mt. Sunflower

The wind blew as a tractor rolled across the dusty ground. A thundercloud promised rain but, like a spook, changed its mind and danced off to the north and then east around the great circle. Grain elevators broke the horizon, often ten or twenty miles away. They stood alone, man-made landmarks, symbols of man's presence.

The sun began to drop behind the rim of the sky and cast growing shadows around us. Alone we watched the pageant of light and clouds gyrating over the flat landscape. Miraculously, rich pinks and lavenders colored the eastern sky long after the luminary had fallen in the west.

Silent, we crossed miles of dark immensity and sought relief from the isolation in a small-town café with a glass of cold tea and a delicious fat hamburger. A group of boisterous hunters was making wild-turkey talk at a round table near us. They seemed curious about the two strangers in the opposite booth and sometimes jabbered to one another, looking over their shoulders at us. They needed no more than a nod or a smile to continue their antics. We were accepted with no spoken acknowledgment. None of us dared break the bond with words, to find we had nothing to talk about except the weather or the loneliness.

Before we finished our simple meal, our host, the owner, tuned his electric guitar and started his steady percussion section. His music pacified us. For a brief time the shells of strangeness cracked and friends gathered to forget the times they feel lonely.

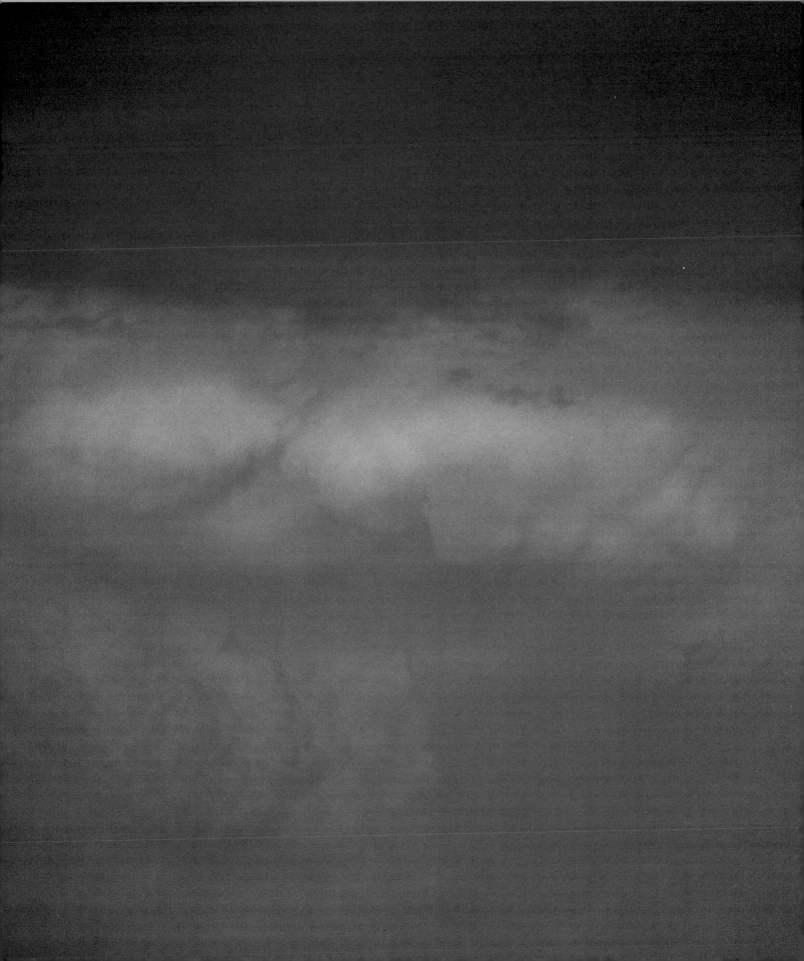

Finding Mt. Sunflower

In the morning the satellite moon rose just before the sun. Crescent in shape, it marked the beginning of another day and the end of its own phase. Like the High Plains, it is both constant and changeable and, for the people who watch it, a companion and a symbol of loneliness.

With the sunrise the land changed again. I marveled at the sand dunes stretching across the fields into the ditches, and I could hide in the early-morning shadows of yucca as tall as trees. The sand dunes displayed fragile ripples and the tracks of many creatures, leaving delicate designs on the fine slopes.

In the Cimarron National Grassland, I broke off a sprig of sagebrush and smelled the pungent odor while eying openings in the ground, homes of animals and insects. The ten o'clock sun warmed the sandy soil and parched the flowers that I dared not pick because they would wilt at the touch of fingertips. When we drove on, I was torn from my reverie as we discovered another kind of reality, oil rigs and tank batteries.

Finding Mt. Sunflower

We searched for Wagon Bed Springs at the confluence of the North Fork and the Cimarron River and found a marker saying ". . .two miles west of here," and ". . .Jedediah Smith was killed by the Indians before reaching the water after four days of searching for the spring." The man who owned the now-dry spring explained that the marker is next to a favorite Indian campsite.

Farther north near the ruins of the El Cuartelejo Indian village, I sipped water from a spring that came out of one of the cliffs surrounding the valley. Then I stood at the top of a cliff and followed the road with my eyes to the horizon, where the earth melted into the sky; a piece of the great circle disappeared, too far away to see.

On the western border of Kansas, we stopped at Mount Sunflower. Except for the scrawled sign at the gate of the pasture, there was no way to tell that this is the highest point in Kansas. In the vastness, one hill appeared to be no higher or lower than the next. At first I laughed, then I was struck with the austerity of the hand-crafted sunflower and the skull that lay near its iron stem. The wind rushed around a dead tree, empty and alone. The surroundings were so barren and lonely that I began to lose my sense of rational proportion. The desolate landscape and the primitive artistic creation on Mount Sunflower's summit were as expressive of my own sense of solitude as any work of art I have experienced.

Wellington-McPherson Lowlands

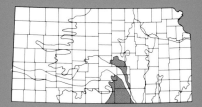

Man must use his heart, mind, and soul in the practice of his craft to elevate it to art.

The Wellington-McPherson Lowlands, divided by the Arkansas River, lie in south-central Kansas. The level terrain; the deep, fertile soil; and the moderate climate make the area very adaptable to wheat and sorghum production. In the irrigated areas, corn and soybeans are grown. Because the region is on the western edge of the flow of moisture from the Gulf of Mexico, rainfall is usually adequate, but occasional years of prolonged dry weather do occur.

McPherson, Newton, and Wellington are the major cities in the area. These cities and most towns are thriving, their economies well balanced with agriculture, petroleum, and industrial enterprises.

Settlers arrived in large numbers in the 1870's, among them Mennonites from Russia, who introduced a variety of hard wheat called Turkey Red to Kansas. A solid, uninterrupted farming base has provided economic stability in this area.

Oil exploration began in the late 1920's, and oil is still an abundant resource. West of McPherson, near Conway, man-made underground salt caverns are used for storing petroleum reserves.

The landscape is consistent, with few surprises. As a rule, country roads are laid out on a one-mile grid system, often making it possible to drive twenty or thirty miles without a turn. Farmsteads and fields are well kept, changing with the seasons from brown, to green, to gold.

Since most of the land is in cultivation, little native plant life remains, but farmsteads, stream beds, and fence rows provide space for the cottonwood, Osage orange, elm, ash, cedar, and many other trees. Most households in town and in the country have small gardens and flower beds, providing food and color. Pheasants, squirrels, rabbits, songbirds, and even deer have adapted to this environment.

Opposite: Kansas produces 20 to 25 percent of the wheat grown in the United States. Left: An old red barn south of Canton; milk cans are symbols of a time past. Below: Rhode Island Reds; work clothes being dried the old-fashioned way.

Farm Country

Kansas is the breadbasket of the United States and perhaps of the world. The Wellington-McPherson Lowlands are in the heart of Kansas; Sumner County, along the southern border of Kansas, is the largest wheat-producing county. In short, this is farming country.

Since I live on a farm in this area, writing about it is like looking into a mirror and describing what I see. I find, as most people do, that it is easier to see someone else's environment with candor and appreciation than it is to appraise my own.

The time has come to say good-bye to Grandfather's farm, except in memory. The pastoral images of barns full of hay, geese and ducks in the yard, and wash on the line are gone. Still, when city friends come to visit, they say, "How peaceful; this is wonderful."

Farm Country

The last decade, during which the family farm has evolved into a complex business, has been difficult for many farmers. As a way of life, farming has changed so drastically that the people involved in it can no longer depend upon the simple way of life their parents and grandparents taught them.

Farming has become an efficiently managed business, as fast-paced as any urban business of equal size. As many hours are spent near a telephone, paper and pencil in hand, as out in the field. Challenges of marketing, planning the year's crops, updating accounting books, and calculating cash flow with a computer fill the office hours, especially in the winter. Since the office is in the home, family life is sometimes interrupted with business affairs.

Opposite top: Binders bind the wheat with twine; the binder reel sweeps the wheat into the sickle; binders were used before the invention of the combine. Opposite below: Wheat is grown in every physiographic region of Kansas. Left: Thresher demonstration; the threshing crew boss. Below: Cutting wheat with a binder; placing the bundles in shocks.

Farming was once much more of a community undertaking. Fifty years ago, when the threshing machine was used, twenty or so neighbors worked together with one harvesting machine. Everyone joined in getting the crop out of the fields and safely stored for the winter. The days were long, but the camaraderie made it easier.

The noon meal was a welcome break from the hard physical labor. Wash basins were filled with water and set outside with towels and soap on low benches. The table was long and laden with fried chicken, fried ham, mashed potatoes, plenty of gravy, beans, corn, dark bread, homemade butter, and jelly. For dessert there was usually fruit pie: apple, peach, apricot, or mulberry-rhubarb. The conversation, between mouthfuls of food, was lively with stories of the morning's events and with plans for the rest of the day. There were rarely any leftovers.

Farm Country

Now, farmers own their own equipment for harvesting or hire it done by custom cutters. Whether the crop is wheat, sorghum, soybeans, or corn, there is little occasion for working shoulder to shoulder to get the job done. Still, it is not unusual for farmers to compare notes, learning from each other in order to improve their efficiency.

Very few farms function as we choose to remember them, with a large barn housing cattle or sheep, a shed for hogs, another for chickens, a nearby pasture for grazing the animals, and small fields with a diversity of crops. Instead, there are large complexes for storing grain, a shop building for repairing the equipment, and a steel building for storing the machines to keep them looking new. The equipment is large because the farms and the fields are large. No longer can a farmer make a living from two or three hundred acres. Farms that are successful now have doubled, tripled, or quadrupled in size in the last ten years.

Opposite: Large silos on a dairy farm in McPherson County. Left: Harvesting corn. Below: A farm boy riding with his dad; the older generation. Bottom: Planting corn.

No matter where we live, most of us have roots in the farm, and all of us depend upon the farm for our food. The peace our city friends feel at our farm occurs partially because we live away from the noise and activity of the city, not because the pressures are fewer or the tension less acute.

Like his counterparts in industry, the farmer maintains a kind of flexible control of his projects. He organizes his day with Murphy's law in mind. Long hours are spent solving the problems that arise: broken machinery, cattle outside of fences, the intrusion of insects, and countless others. He manages the crop year with the knowledge that the weather is an unknown factor to which he must continually adapt.

At times, his family must change plans quickly when there is a crisis. On the other hand, when the workload eases unexpectedly there is a special trip to town to see friends or to enjoy an evening of recreation. Most successful farmers maintain a sense of humor. One said the other day, with a sly smile, "I'm afraid it might rain, and then again I'm afraid it won't."

Many farmers, like good craftsmen, set high standards for themselves. They take pride in their work by planting straight rows, mowing the ditches around their fields, and keeping their farmsteads in meticulous order.

Regardless of the business-like quality of the farm, there are still pastures with cattle grazing peacefully and rivers with chattering cottonwoods. Sometimes a herd of deer can be seen in the early morning, and a coyote may race across the field as if embarrassed to be seen. There is the chance of finding a baby jack rabbit and showing it to the children. There is time to take a few minutes for a hot meal in the field.

There is pleasure in watching the planted seeds sprout and grow, covering the brown earth with rows of tiny green plants. At times, it hardly seems like work to nurse the fields to maturity and then to harvest them, to see the golden wheat, and to smell the freshly cut straw. One need only look into the eyes of a farmer as he holds kernels of grain, his harvest, to share the joy of his craft.

Opposite top: The straight-planted rows of corn on an irrigation field. Opposite below: Cottonwoods grow as tall as 100 feet. Left: A farmer's watchdog; a herd of Simmental-Hereford cross cattle; alfalfa bales weigh about seventy pounds each. Below: Large round bales are stacked for winter feeding.

Left: Kansas's largest natural lake, Lake Inman. Below: Combining soybeans at dusk. Right: Winter king crab berries covered with ice; a red-tailed hawk. Opposite top: A group of well-tended daisies; red oak leaves in the fall. Opposite below: A rainbow after the storm.

The meadowlark greets the early riser, and the hawk is a constant companion high above. Seagulls circle the freshly turned earth in the springtime, and, after a sweltering day, the thunderclouds may roll in. In the fall, geese and ducks flying south announce the end of another busy season, and winter brings a time to reflect on the year's activity.

The excitement the settlers must have felt in developing new lands is gone. The adventure of man against the elements is fast disappearing. Technology is making new demands, and it is another kind of adventure that faces us. It remains to be seen whether we have the intelligence, the fortitude, the love, the care, and the ability to face the next hundred years with a sense of adventure, or whether we will let what we have built govern us.

Smoky Hills

Wisdom arises from man's appreciation and knowledge of his relationship to a flower, a fossil, or a sunrise.

The Smoky Hills region bridges the eastern and western parts of the state. Annual rainfall ranges from an average of twenty-eight inches in the eastern Smoky Hills to nineteen inches in the west. Tall grass gives way to short grass as the terrain gradually ascends to the High Plains.

Geologically, the region has three types of terrain on ascending levels of elevation. In the east are the sandstone outcrops, typified by Coronado Heights, near Lindsborg. In the middle is limestone country, where stone fence posts line the fields and roads. In the west thick layers of chalk produce such landmarks as Castle Rock in Gove County.

European exploration began here with Coronado's trek in 1541. After that, there is no record of white activity until the early 1800's, when fur hunters and trail explorers penetrated the area. Fort Ellsworth was established in 1864 and Fort Hays in 1865. Salina, in 1864, consisted of three residences, one store, a hotel, and a blacksmith shop. By 1867 the Kansas Pacific Railroad had reached Ellsworth, and for about four years it was one of the roughest cattle towns in Kansas.

Agriculturally, wheat and livestock dominate the area. Salina and Hays have attracted a variety of industries, many petroleum related. The region appears stable, prosperous, and proud, its spirit represented in the small city of Lindsborg, with its college, museum, noted art gallery, and unique city center.

Six reservoirs, a dozen flowing rivers, and thousands of acres of grassland provide opportunities for year-round outdoor recreation, including hunting and fishing. Colorful local festivals and celebrations, like the Czech Festival in Wilson, attract wide interest.

In the Sea

This journey began at dawn near a wheat field in Saline County. From a hilltop, patches of ground fog were visible in the lowlands, and other hilltops looked like islands in a sea of gray vapor.

Just before sunrise, the sky blazed kaleidoscopic red and orange, changing constantly. Then, as quickly as they had come, the colors disappeared, and the new light disclosed the smoky haze which gives the region its name. As the sun rose higher, the fog burned away and revealed an undulating ocean of pale green wheat in the field below us.

Our attention was caught by a variety of wildflowers: white asters, soap weed (commonly called yucca), and catclaw sensitivebriar. As we admired them, a small lizard, sunning himself on a ledge in the Dakota sandstone, stared at us. For a moment we stood eye to eye; being so close to us, this small, green reptile appeared much larger and seemed about to pounce on us. Suddenly, he scurried back into his hole in the granular rocks.

Dakota sandstone is quartz sand that one hundred million years ago was a beach on the shore of a shallow sea. Over millions of years, the grains of sand were pressed together, forming sandstone. Blocks of the reddish-brown Dakota sandstone were used in the building of the Fort Harker guard house at Kanopolis and the lookout tower at Coronado Heights, as well as in many other buildings in the area.

Near Minneapolis, we found Rock City, strange outcroppings of giant sandstone spheres scattered over the hillside. These configurations, some over twenty-seven feet in diameter, seemed like misplaced pieces of moon rock. They are made up of quartz grains cemented around calcite crystals. Water has eroded the softer surrounding sandstone, leaving the spherical formations.

Opposite top: The lookout tower at Coronado Heights. Opposite below: A cluster of round rocks at Rock City near Minneapolis. Right: A mushroom rock in a park near Kanopolis Reservoir; a Dakota sandstone rock formation. Below: Some of the sandstone rocks are up to 27 feet in diameter.

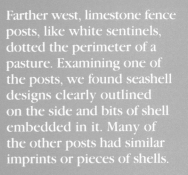

Opposite: A limestone fencepost braced for a gate. Left: The spires of the St. Fidelis Church; a fossil shell embedded in limestone. Below: Limestone fence posts outlast the barbed wire; fossils are tangible evidence of life long ago.

In the Sea

Farther west, limestone fence posts, like white sentinels, dotted the perimeter of a pasture. Examining one of the posts, we found seashell designs clearly outlined on the side and bits of shell embedded in it. Many of the other posts had similar imprints or pieces of shells.

A farmer working in a nearby field stopped his tractor for a moment to talk to us. He told us that his father had helped cut fence posts out of the horizontal outcropping of limestone several miles away. The topsoil had been removed from above the eight-to-ten-inch stratum of limestone. Quickly, before the rock hardened, holes had been drilled by hand every eight to ten inches and then wedges driven into the holes to break the stone loose. "My father helped cut the stone for the St. Fidelis church, too," he said proudly. "While the stone was still soft, they could carve it to the exact dimensions needed." He pointed westward and we saw the two spires of the church, also known as the Cathedral of the Plains, against the horizon. His story told, the farmer went back to his work, and we hadn't the time to ask if he shared our enthusiasm for the shell imprints in the fence posts.

The limestone layers were formed later than the Dakota sandstone. They had once been at the bottom of a shallow sea and contained the remnants of billions of shellfish in fossil form. Fossilized sharks' teeth, remains of sharks some thirty feet in length, can also be found in the limestone rocks. Giant squid up to sixty feet long and huge clams also inhabited the water.

In the Sea

From the limestone rock country we traveled to Castle Rock and the Chalk Pyramids in Gove County to see the youngest of the geological formations in the Smoky Hill Region. All these formations began in the Cretaceous Period, which lasted seventy-five million years.

Nature has left large and stately chalk formations on the prairies. At the Castle Rock site, an upland pasture dropped suddenly into rugged badlands to the south and flat pastureland to the north, where Castle Rock towered over thirty feet high. The Chalk Pyramids, on the other side of the county, were reminiscent of Stonehenge, only much larger and more numerous.

Castle Rock and the Chalk Pyramids were formed from microscopic plants and animals that lived in the last of the great seas which covered Kansas. Layer upon layer was formed as this marine life died and filtered to the bottom, creating chalk beds up to seven hundred fifty feet thick. When the Rocky Mountains pushed out of the earth's surface, the Smoky Hill River began to sculpt the formations we see today. Large fossils, some of them on display in the Smithsonian Institution in Washington, D. C., have been found in these chalk beds.

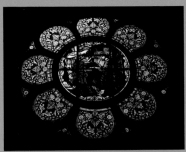

Opposite top: The old Cawker City library; Pete Felten's "Monarch of the Plains," sculpted from limestone; Waconda Lake. Opposite below: Hillside near Lake Wilson. Left: Purple poppymallows blooming in Rock City; stained glass window of St. Fidelis Church in Victoria. Below: St. Fidelis; Church in Pfeifer; church in Catherine.

In the Sea

At the Sternberg Museum on the Fort Hays State University campus, we found many fossils from the Smoky Hill Region. These fossils date back to the Cretaceous Period, sixty million to one hundred forty million years ago, when the dinosaur lived among flying reptiles, birds with teeth, and huge turtles.

Now when we travel through the Smoky Hills, we search for signs of the earth's ancient past. At Waconda Lake, where the chalky shores flash against the blue water, we see pelicans and blue herons that are similar in many ways to the birds and flying reptiles from the Cretaceous Period. As we drive the country roads in post-rock country, we seek out the fence posts with unusual impressions of ancient sea life. We search the ground for rocks that contain fossils. We have learned to distinguish the different kinds of rocks that represent different parts of the story of ancient Kansas.

When we see the magnificent churches, especially in the Hays area, and the sandstone buildings near Kanopolis, we have a new appreciation of the stone from which they are constructed. Even the roadside rock strata, exposed when cuts are made in the hills, tell us of the past.

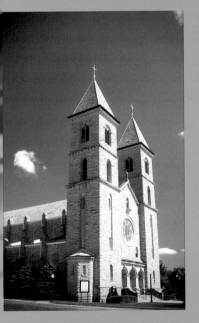

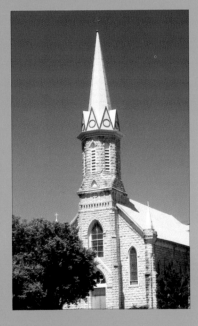

From Horse Thief Canyon near Kanopolis Reservoir to the sandstone building on top of Coronado Heights, from the outcroppings near Wilson Reservoir to the chalky lands of the Upper Smoky River basin, from the Mushroom Rocks to the green lizard that peers from its ledge, the alert traveler finds evidence of an exciting, evolving world.

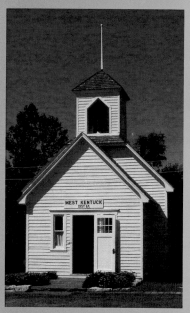

Opposite top: Pricklypoppy with grasshopper; large concretions of Dakota sandstone. Opposite below: Christmas in Lyons; West Kentuck School in Lindsborg. Left: Kansas is noted for its blue skies; western salsify looks like a giant dandelion; alfalfa drying in windrows. Below: A view of Coronado Heights. Page 128: A Smoky Hills panorama.